MILITARY AIRCRAFT
AH-64D APACHE
LONGBOW
BY JOHN HAMILTON

VISIT US AT
WWW.ABDOPUBLISHING.COM

Published by ABDO Publishing Company, PO Box 398166, Minneapolis, MN 55439.
Copyright ©2012 by Abdo Consulting Group, Inc. International copyrights reserved in all countries. No part of this book may be reproduced in any form without written permission from the publisher. A&D Xtreme™ is a trademark and logo of ABDO Publishing Company.

Printed in the United States of America, North Mankato, Minnesota.
122011
012012

PRINTED ON RECYCLED PAPER

Editor: Sue Hamilton
Graphic Design: Sue Hamilton
Cover Design: John Hamilton
Cover Photo: iStockphoto
Interior Photos: Boeing-pgs 1, 6-7, 10-11, 20-21, 26-27 & 32; Corbis-pgs 16-17 & 28-29; Defense Video & Imagery Distribution System-pgs 12-13, 19 (inset), 22-23, & 25 (inset); Getty Images-pgs 8-9 & 24-25; ThinkStock-pgs 2-3, 4-5, 14-15, 18-19 & 30-31.

ABDO Booklinks
Web sites about Military Aircraft are featured on our Book Links pages. These links are routinely monitored and updated to provide the most current information available.
Web site: www.abdopublishing.com

Library of Congress Cataloging-in-Publication Data

Hamilton, John, 1959-
 AH-64D Apache Longbow / John Hamilton.
    p. cm. -- (Xtreme military aircraft)
 Includes index.
 ISBN 978-1-61783-266-6
 1. Apache (Attack helicopter)--Juvenile literature. I. Title.
 UG1232.A88H35 2012
 623.74'63--dc23
                                    2011042346

TABLE OF CONTENTS

AH-64D APACHE
LONGBOW ★★★

The AH-64D Apache Longbow is an attack helicopter. It is used by the United States Army. With its advanced radar and missiles, the Apache Longbow is one of the most dangerous weapons on the modern battlefield.

XTREME FACT

The Apache Longbow is sometimes called a flying tank. It survives heavy attacks. It also delivers massive firepower upon enemy forces. It is a terrifying weapon of war.

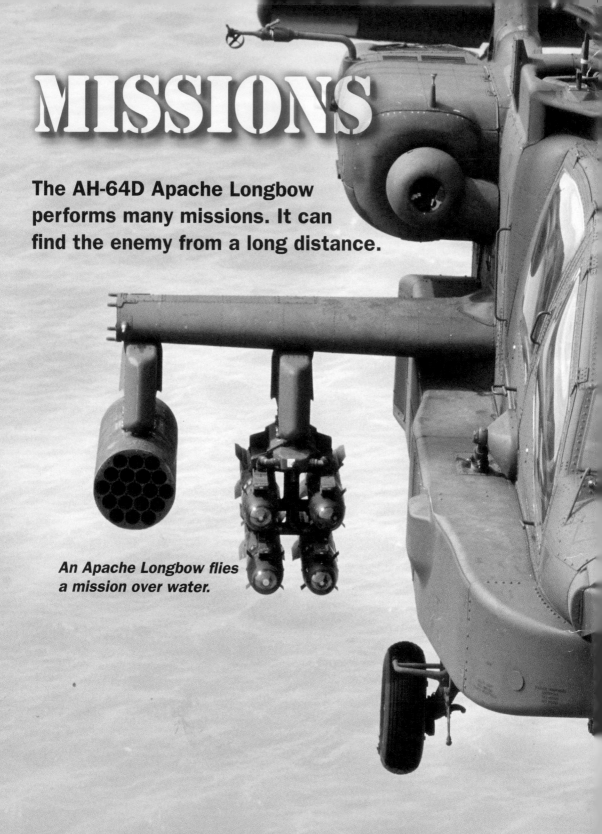

MISSIONS

The AH-64D Apache Longbow performs many missions. It can find the enemy from a long distance.

An Apache Longbow flies a mission over water.

The Apache Longbow can attack day or night, in good or bad weather. It is especially good at destroying tanks and other armored vehicles.

XTREME FACT

The United States Army has about 800 AH-64D Apache Longbows in service.

ORIGINS

The first Apache helicopters were designed in the late 1970s and early 1980s. The U.S. Army wanted to replace its fleet of aging AH-1 Cobra helicopters. The Army wanted fast, powerful helicopters that could destroy enemy tanks.

An Apache helicopter fires a Hydra 70 rocket over northern Iraq.

The first Apache helicopters were used in combat when the United States invaded Panama in 1989. Since then, updated Apaches have used new technology. The AH-64D Apache Longbow is the latest version. It entered service in the late 1990s.

XTREME FACT

More than 1,000 Apache Longbows are used by America's allies, including the United Kingdom, Israel, Kuwait, Japan, and the Netherlands.

AH-64D APACHE LONGBOW FAST FACTS

The Apache Longbow is highly maneuverable. Fully loaded, it can perform loops, 360-degree turns, and left and right rolls.

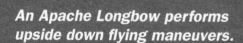

An Apache Longbow performs upside down flying maneuvers.

AH-64D Apache Longbow Specifications

Function:	Attack Helicopter
Service Branch:	United States Army
Manufacturer:	Boeing
Length:	58.2 feet (17.7 m)
Height:	15.2 feet (4.6 m)
Crew:	2 (pilot and co-pilot/gunner)
Weight:	15,075 pounds (6,838 kg)
Speed:	173 miles per hour (278 kph)
Combat Range:	300 miles (483 km)

ENGINES

An AH-64D Apache Longbow engine.

The Apache Longbow uses two General Electric T700-GE-701 turboshaft engines. They are powerful and reliable. They are mounted on each side of the helicopter's fuselage.

Hot gasses flowing through the turboshaft engines turn turbine wheels. They are connected to a transmission system, which spins the helicopter's rotor blades.

ROTORS

The Apache Longbow uses a four-blade main rotor and tail rotor.

The newest Apache Longbow model has a blade that is very strong. It is made of a graphite composite material. It also has a stainless steel leading edge.

XTREME FACT

The Apache Longbow's main rotor is strong enough to withstand small-arms fire, or brushes with trees and other obstacles when flying low.

The diameter of the full main rotor is 48 feet (14.6 m).

CREW

The Apache Longbow cockpit has two compartments. The pilot sits in back. The compartment is raised to give the pilot a better view. The pilot uses digital displays that show navigation systems and flight information.

The co-pilot sits in front in an Apache Longbow. The co-pilot is also the gunner, in charge of aiming and firing the weapons.

SENSORS

The Apache Longbow uses the Longbow Fire Control Radar system. It is located in a dome above the main rotor blades. It gathers and processes battlefield information. It sends target data to the crew in seconds.

Other sensors include laser rangefinders, night vision sensors, and TV optical sensors. Much of this information is projected on a small screen in front of the pilot or gunner's right eye.

TARGETING

A pilot uses an Apache Longbow's full color multi-purpose display.

The Apache Longbow's sensors and optics can identify up to 128 enemy targets, such as tanks. Sixteen of the most dangerous threats are given top priority. This data can be sent to other helicopters. The entire group can then launch a precision attack in less than one minute.

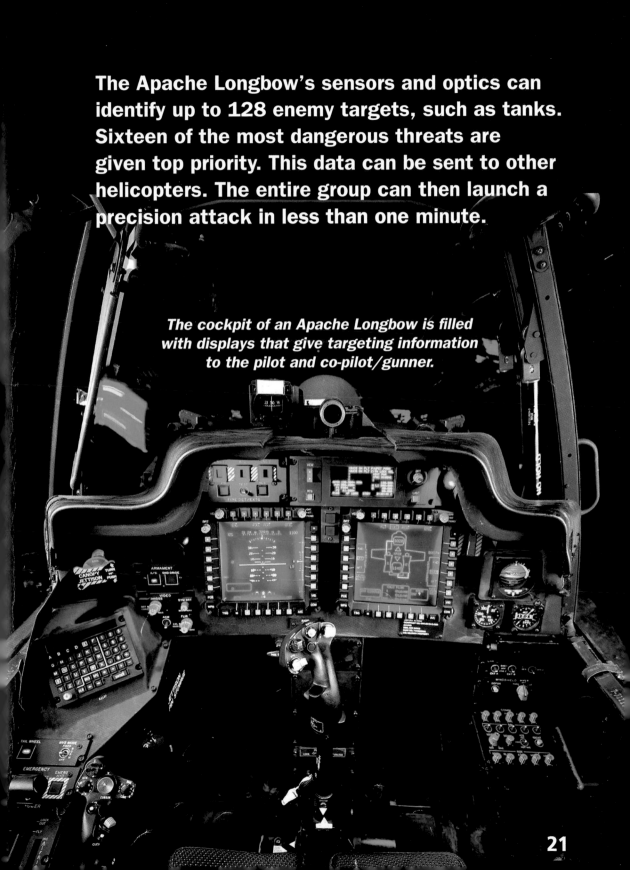

The cockpit of an Apache Longbow is filled with displays that give targeting information to the pilot and co-pilot/gunner.

MISSILES

A Hellfire missile attached to an Apache Longbow.

The Apache Longbow can carry 16 AGM-114 Hellfire missiles. They are attached to stub-wing pylons on either side of the fuselage. Newer Hellfire missiles use radar instead of lasers to lock onto their targets. Each missile can easily destroy an enemy tank.

XTREME FACT

For defense against enemy aircraft, the Apache Longbow carries Stinger or Sidewinder air-to-air missiles.

OTHER WEAPONS

The Apache Longbow can carry Hydra 70 rocket pods. They are mounted on each side of the helicopter. Up to 38 70mm rockets can be fired at one time. These unguided missiles are sometimes used against enemy infantry.

The Apache Longbow's M230 30mm chain gun is mounted under the fuselage. It shoots 625 rounds per minute. The high-explosive rounds can pierce light armor.

The M230 chain gun can be controlled by the pilot's helmet display. It automatically aims wherever the pilot is looking. The chain gun can also automatically track moving targets.

DEFENSE

The Apache Longbow avoids the enemy by attacking from far away. It can hover behind trees or low hills. It can also electronically jam enemy radar and missiles.

The Apache
Longbow is
designed to be tough.
The crew compartment is
protected by steel, Kevlar, and
bulletproof glass. Critical systems, such
as the engines and rotors, are also protected.

COMBAT
HISTORY

The AH-64D Apache Longbow has fought in several wars. It has recently been used in combat in Iraq and Afghanistan. The Apache Longbow is a feared battlefield weapon. It will be used by the U.S. Army for many years to come.

GLOSSARY

ARMOR
A strong, protective covering made to protect military vehicles.

ATTACK HELICOPTER
A helicopter used in an offensive battlefield role, such as attacking troops or destroying tanks. Other types of helicopters specialize in transporting troops and equipment, spying on the enemy, or evacuating wounded soldiers.

CHAIN GUN
An automatic cannon that is similar to a machine gun, except it is powered by an electric motor. The motor rotates a chain, which allows the gun to load, fire, and eject spent cartridges rapidly.

INFANTRY
Soldiers who move and fight mainly on foot.

KEVLAR
A light and very strong man-made fiber. It is used to make helmets, vests, and other protective gear for military and law enforcement personnel.

NAVIGATION SYSTEM
A computer and satellite system that provides directions and locations.

RADAR
A way to detect objects, such as aircraft or ships, using electromagnetic (radio) waves. Radar waves are sent out by large dishes, or antennas, and then strike an object. The radar dish then detects the reflected wave, which can tell operators how big an object is, how fast it is moving, its altitude, and its direction.

TRANSMISSION
A system of gears and other mechanical devices that transfers the power from an engine to the wheels of a vehicle, or rotor of a helicopter.

INDEX